IRISH SIGNS
AND NOTICES

IRISH SIGNS AND NOTICES

DES MacHALE

MERCIER PRESS

Irish Publisher – Irish Story

MERCIER PRESS

Cork

www.mercierpress.ie

Trade enquiries to CMD BookSource,
55a Spruce Avenue, Stillorgan Industrial Park,
Blackrock, County Dublin

© Des MacHale, 2010

ISBN: 978 1 85635 658 9

10 9 8 7 6 5 4 3 2 1

A CIP record for this title is available from the British Library

Printed and bound in the EU.

Introduction

What is it about a sign or a notice that often provokes hilarity? The message is condensed, space is at a premium, and the sign or notice often loses its meaning, or indeed acquires a whole new meaning, sometimes unintended, and in many delicious cases, quite rude.

To put this book together I have scoured toilets (not literally!), hotels, churches, shops and supermarkets, garage forecourts, car stickers, undertakers (surprisingly funny), pubs and bars, buses, trains, factories, schools and colleges, farms, newspapers, sports clubs, and indeed just about anywhere signs and notices are displayed in Ireland. The results, I think you will agree, are hilarious and add yet another dimension to Irish humour, already known to be the best in the world. This collection of nearly 400 hilariously funny signs and notices is the biggest collection ever assembled. All are of course absolutely authentic – and if you believe that, you'll believe anything!

Enjoy.

Des MacHale

At a barber's shop

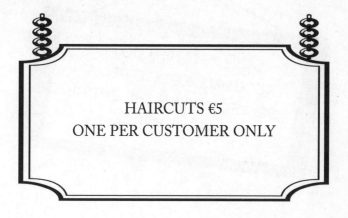

HAIRCUTS €5
ONE PER CUSTOMER ONLY

At a beauty parlour

EARS PIERCED
WHILE YOU WAIT

PAY FOR TWO
GET ONE DONE FREE

In a toilet

LADIES IN THIS LOO ARE RECOMMENDED TO REMAIN SEATED DURING THE ENTIRE PERFORMANCE

In a student hall of residence

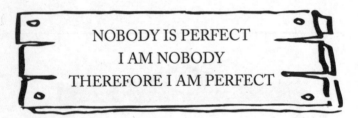

NOBODY IS PERFECT
I AM NOBODY
THEREFORE I AM PERFECT

On a house

THE DOG IS FRIENDLY
BEWARE OF THE WIFE

In a bathroom

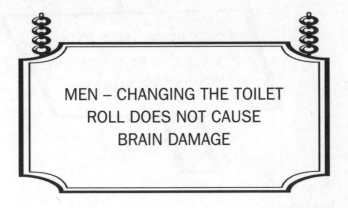

MEN – CHANGING THE TOILET
ROLL DOES NOT CAUSE
BRAIN DAMAGE

Near a swimming pool

SHARKS HAVE BEEN SPOTTED
IN THIS POOL
THEY COME OUT ONLY
WHEN THEY SMELL PEE

In a railway station

TOILET OUT OF ORDER
PLEASE USE PLATFORMS
TWO AND THREE

In a factory

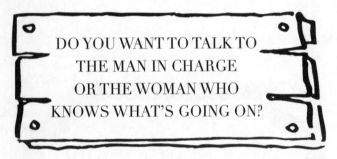

DO YOU WANT TO TALK TO
THE MAN IN CHARGE
OR THE WOMAN WHO
KNOWS WHAT'S GOING ON?

On a farm gate

WE SHOOT EVERY TENTH
TRESPASSER
THE NINTH ONE HAS JUST LEFT

THIS SHOP IS CLOSED
FOR YOUR
CONVENIENCE

OUR VACUUM CLEANERS
REALLY SUCK

OUR BIKINIS ARE
JUST TOPS

JUNK WANTED

ANTIQUES FOR SALE

FOR THOSE WHO LIKE HAGGLING, WE WILL GLADLY RAISE THE PRICE SO WE CAN GIVE YOU A DISCOUNT

BARGAIN BASEMENT
UPSTAIRS

WE EXCHANGE ANYTHING:
BICYCLES, FRIDGES, BAGS.
WHY NOT BRING YOUR WIFE
ALONG AND GET A WONDERFUL
BARGAIN?

YOUR HUSBAND JUST CALLED
AND SAID YOU CAN BUY
ANYTHING YOU WANT

NO SMOKING
GUIDE DOGS EXCEPTED

THESE BELTS WILL LAST
FOREVER AND AFTERWARDS
CAN BE USED FOR LUGGAGE

UNATTENDED CHILDREN
WILL BE GIVEN A LOLLIPOP
AND A FREE PUPPY

HUSBANDS BUYING
PAINT MUST HAVE
NOTE FROM WIFE

THREE SANTA CLAUSES
NO WAITING

T-BONES €1
WITH MEAT €10

TROUSERS €10
THEY WON'T LAST LONG AT
THIS PRICE

MOTHERS ARE REQUESTED
NOT TO LEAVE THEIR
CHILDREN SITTING ON THE
BACON SLICER AS WE ARE
GETTING A LITTLE
BEHIND WITH OUR ORDERS

A SMALL DEPOSIT SECURES
ANY ITEM UNTIL YOU CAN
PERSUADE YOUR HUSBAND

OUR STAFF ARE ON STRIKE
BUSINESS AS USUAL DURING
ALTERCATIONS

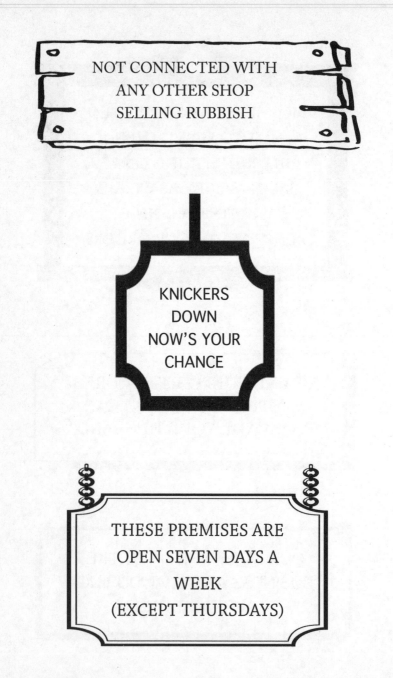

NOT CONNECTED WITH
ANY OTHER SHOP
SELLING RUBBISH

KNICKERS
DOWN
NOW'S YOUR
CHANCE

THESE PREMISES ARE
OPEN SEVEN DAYS A
WEEK
(EXCEPT THURSDAYS)

OUR NYLONS ARE EXPENSIVE
BUT WORTH IT IN THE LONG RUN

UNATTENDED
CHILDREN
WILL BE SOLD
INTO SLAVERY

OPEN TWENTY-FOUR
HOURS A DAY
LONGER AT WEEKENDS

DON'T BE CHEATED ELSEWHERE
COME IN HERE

CLOSED ON ACCOUNT
OF RE-OPENING

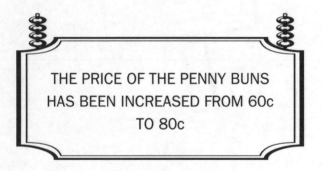

THE PRICE OF THE PENNY BUNS
HAS BEEN INCREASED FROM 60c
TO 80c

NO DISSATISFIED
CUSTOMER IS
EVER ALLOWED TO
LEAVE THIS SHOP

YES WE ARE OPEN –
PLEASE CALL
BACK AT SOME OTHER TIME

THESE ARE PURE
WOOL CARDIGANS.
THE LABEL SAYS
COTTON JUST TO
FOOL THE MOTHS

IN GOD WE TRUST
ALL OTHERS PAY CASH

OUR EGGS
CANNOT
BE BEATEN

On a public toilet

INCOMING TRAFFIC
HAS THE RIGHT OF WAY

In a house

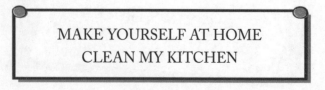

MAKE YOURSELF AT HOME
CLEAN MY KITCHEN

In a launderette

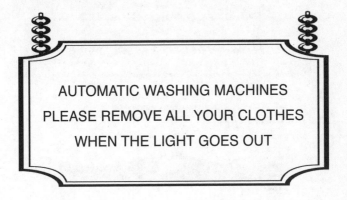

AUTOMATIC WASHING MACHINES
PLEASE REMOVE ALL YOUR CLOTHES
WHEN THE LIGHT GOES OUT

In a toilet

In an auction room

WET FLOOR
(THIS IS
NOT AN
INSTRUCTION)

THE HIGHEST
BIDDER TO BE
THE PURCHASER –
UNLESS SOMEBODY
BIDS MORE

On a health food shop

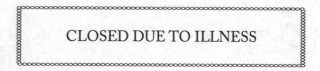

CLOSED DUE TO ILLNESS

On a publisher's office

OFFICE HOURS
2 TO 2:15 EVERY
OTHER WEDNESDAY

On a photographer's studio

OUT TO LUNCH
IF NOT BACK BY FIVE
OUT TO DINNER ALSO

On a repair shop door

WE CAN REPAIR ANYTHING
(PLEASE KNOCK HARD ON
THE DOOR AS THE BELL
DOES NOT WORK)

On a dance hall

LADIES AND GENTLEMEN
WELCOME
REGARDLESS OF SEX

On a pet shop

PLEASE DO NOT FONDLE
THE ANIMALS
ASK FOR MAUREEN

On an antique shop

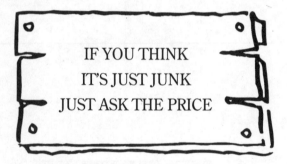

IF YOU THINK
IT'S JUST JUNK
JUST ASK THE PRICE

On an advertising hoarding

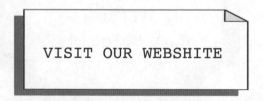

VISIT OUR WEBSHITE

JUST BECAUSE YOUR DOCTOR
TOLD YOU THAT YOU NEED
GLASSES THERE'S
NO NEED TO STEAL OURS

FREE BEER HERE ALL NEXT WEEK
TO CUSTOMERS OVER
NINETY PROVIDED THEY ARE
ACCOMPANIED BY THEIR
GRANDPARENTS

WE HAVE A SPECIAL ARRANGEMENT
WITH THE BANKS
THEY DON'T SELL BEER
WE DON'T CASH CHEQUES

BEER – HELPING UGLY
PEOPLE TO HAVE SEX
SINCE 1800

IN CASE OF FIRE PLEASE PAY
FOR YOUR DRINKS IMMEDIATELY

DON'T TAKE THE PISS OUT
OF OUR BEER
IT NEEDS ALL THE
FLAVOUR IT CAN GET

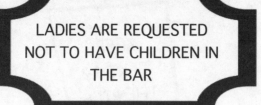

LADIES ARE REQUESTED
NOT TO HAVE CHILDREN IN
THE BAR

NO
ADMITTANCE
UNLESS YOU
WANT TO
COME IN

HELEN WAITE IS OUR
CREDIT MANAGER,
IF YOU WANT CREDIT GO
TO HELEN WAITE

KEEP
TAKING
THE PILS

YOU DON'T HAVE TO
BE CRAZY TO WORK
HERE:
WE'LL TRAIN YOU!

BOOZENESS AS USUAL

BEER –
HELPING WHITE MEN
TO DANCE SINCE 1850

GOOD CLEAN
ENTERTAINMENT IN THIS
PUB EVERY NIGHT
EXCEPT TUESDAY

DRINKING MAY CAUSE MEMORY LOSS
OR WORSE STILL MEMORY LOSS

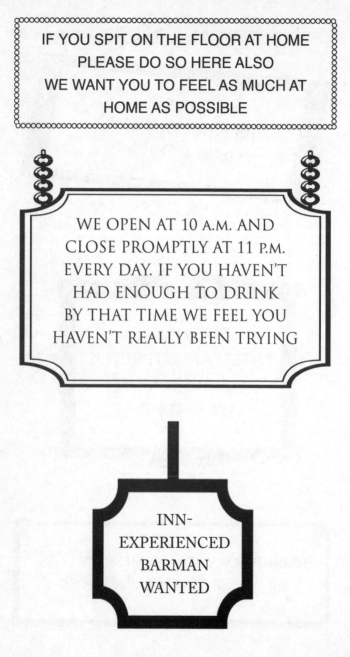

IF YOU SPIT ON THE FLOOR AT HOME
PLEASE DO SO HERE ALSO
WE WANT YOU TO FEEL AS MUCH AT
HOME AS POSSIBLE

WE OPEN AT 10 A.M. AND
CLOSE PROMPTLY AT 11 P.M.
EVERY DAY. IF YOU HAVEN'T
HAD ENOUGH TO DRINK
BY THAT TIME WE FEEL YOU
HAVEN'T REALLY BEEN TRYING

INN-
EXPERIENCED
BARMAN
WANTED

THE MANAGEMENT WILL NOT
BE RESPONSIBLE FOR ANY
INJURIES SUSTAINED IN THE
MAD RUSH FOR THE DOORS
AT CLOSING TIME

EVERYONE SHOULD BELIEVE IN
SOMETHING
I BELIEVE I'LL HAVE ANOTHER
BEER

PLEASE DO NOT
ASK FOR CREDIT
AS A PUNCH IN
THE MOUTH
OFTEN OFFENDS

PLEASE DO NOT
EAT THE LARGE
POLO MINTS IN
THE URINALS

THE RIVERSIDE PUB IS CLOSED DUE TO THE RIVER BEING INSIDE THE PUB

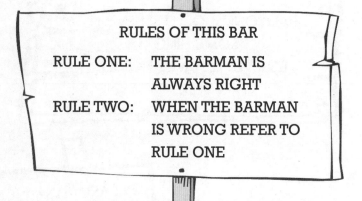

RULES OF THIS BAR

RULE ONE: THE BARMAN IS ALWAYS RIGHT

RULE TWO: WHEN THE BARMAN IS WRONG REFER TO RULE ONE

On a music shop door

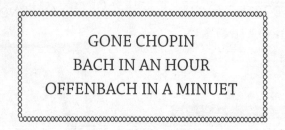

GONE CHOPIN
BACH IN AN HOUR
OFFENBACH IN A MINUET

At a filling station

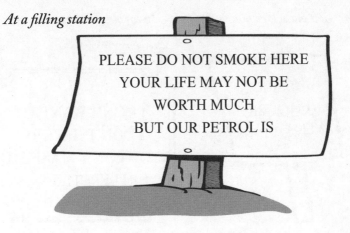

PLEASE DO NOT SMOKE HERE
YOUR LIFE MAY NOT BE
WORTH MUCH
BUT OUR PETROL IS

On an optician's window

IF YOU CANNOT READ THIS
COME INSIDE BECAUSE
YOU MAY NEED SPECTACLES

On a railway crossing

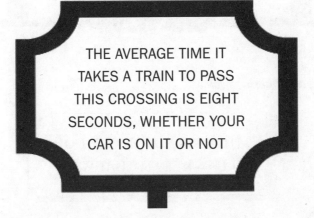

THE AVERAGE TIME IT
TAKES A TRAIN TO PASS
THIS CROSSING IS EIGHT
SECONDS, WHETHER YOUR
CAR IS ON IT OR NOT

In a bachelor's house

A HOME IS
A HOUSE
WITH A BAR

In an old folks' home

I DON'T WANT TO
I DON'T HAVE TO
YOU CAN'T MAKE ME
I'M RETIRED

In a kitchen

I HAVE A KITCHEN ONLY
BECAUSE IT CAME WITH THE
HOUSE

By a swimming pool

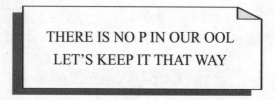

THERE IS NO P IN OUR OOL
LET'S KEEP IT THAT WAY

In a student hall of residence

WHAT IF THE HOKEY COKEY
IS WHAT IT'S ALL ABOUT?

In a launderette

LADIES WHY NOT LEAVE YOUR
CLOTHES HERE AND SPEND THE
AFTERNOON HAVING A GOOD TIME?

On a nightclub

EXCLUSIVE DISCO
EVERYONE
WELCOME

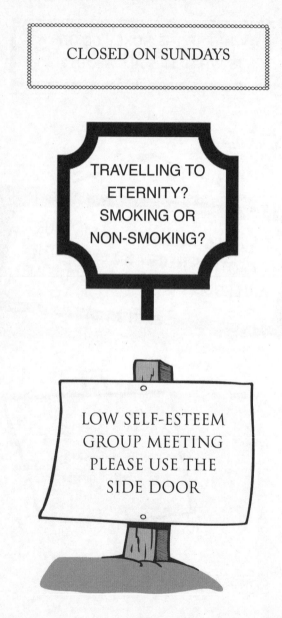

CLOSED ON SUNDAYS

TRAVELLING TO
ETERNITY?
SMOKING OR
NON-SMOKING?

LOW SELF-ESTEEM
GROUP MEETING
PLEASE USE THE
SIDE DOOR

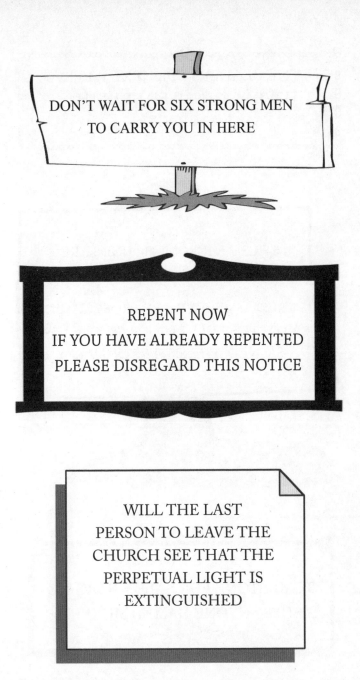

DON'T WAIT FOR SIX STRONG MEN
TO CARRY YOU IN HERE

REPENT NOW
IF YOU HAVE ALREADY REPENTED
PLEASE DISREGARD THIS NOTICE

WILL THE LAST
PERSON TO LEAVE THE
CHURCH SEE THAT THE
PERPETUAL LIGHT IS
EXTINGUISHED

THE READERS FOR NEXT WEEK
HAVE BEEN NAILED UP IN THE
SACRISTY

THESE CHURCH GROUNDS ARE
PRIVATE

TRESPASSERS WILL BE PROSECUTED
WITH THE FULL RIGOUR OF THE LAW
SIGNED: THE SISTERS OF MERCY

TOMBSTONE FOR SALE – BARGAIN
SUIT ANYONE NAMED MURPHY

On a farm gate

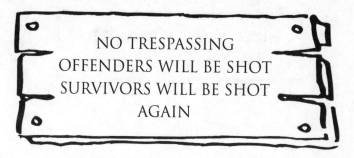

NO TRESPASSING
OFFENDERS WILL BE SHOT
SURVIVORS WILL BE SHOT
AGAIN

On a tombstone

I TOLD YOU
I WAS SICK

On a Dublin bus

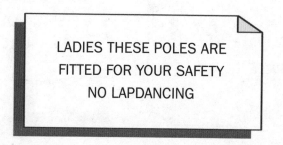

LADIES THESE POLES ARE
FITTED FOR YOUR SAFETY
NO LAPDANCING

On a video rental shop

WHY NOT HIRE A DVD
FOR A DULL EVENING?

In an Indian restaurant

AFTER ONE MEAL HERE WE
GUARANTEE YOU WILL BE
A REGULAR CUSTOMER

On an undertakers

DRIVE CAREFULLY
WE CAN WAIT

Near a lake

BOAT FOR HIRE
FISHING OR
PLEASURE

In a furniture shop

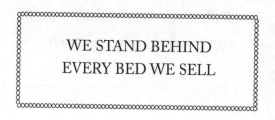

WE STAND BEHIND
EVERY BED WE SELL

At a land fill

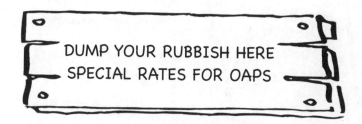

DUMP YOUR RUBBISH HERE
SPECIAL RATES FOR OAPS

On a golf course

LOST BALLS ARE NOT
TO BE PICKED UP UNTIL
THEY HAVE STOPPED
ROLLING

EAT AT THIS RESTAURANT
AND YOU WILL NEVER EAT
ANYWHERE ELSE AGAIN

TOILET FOR
SITTING DOWN
CUSTOMERS
ONLY

ALL-DAY BREAKFAST
SERVED
7.30 A.M.–10.30 A.M.

CUSTOMERS WHO THINK
OUR STAFF ARE BAD-
MANNERED SHOULD SEE
THE MANAGER

ALL WATER IN THESE
PREMISES HAS
BEEN PERSONALLY PASSED
BY THE MANAGER

IF YOU'RE SMOKING
IN HERE, YOU'D BETTER
BE ON FIRE

TOILETS
PLEASE WAIT FOR WAITER
TO SEAT YOU

CLOSED FOR LUNCH

YOU CAN EAT DIRT
CHEAP IN THIS RESTAURANT

WANTED
MAN TO WASH DISHES
AND TWO WAITRESSES

HO LEE FUK
CHINESE
RESTAURANT

OUR MOST
POPULAR
DISH IS TRIPE

100% FRESHLY-SQUEEZED
PURE ORANGE JUICE
FROM CONCENTRATE

WE WILL SHORTLY OPEN A
CAFETERIA WITH COURTEOUS AND
EFFICIENT SELF-SERVICE

MULTIPLE
CHOICE MENU
TAKE IT OR
LEAVE IT

OUR CUTLERY IS NOT
MEDICINE SO PLEASE DO NOT
TAKE IT AFTER MEALS

IF IT FITS IN A TOASTER
WE CAN COOK IT

IN MULDOON'S RESTAURANT
GOOD FOOD IS AN
UNEXPECTED PLEASURE

At a maternity hospital

NO
CHILDREN
ALLOWED

On a traffic sign

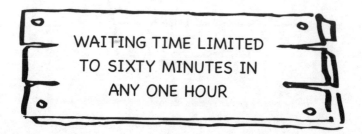

WAITING TIME LIMITED
TO SIXTY MINUTES IN
ANY ONE HOUR

On a road sign

PUBLIC TOILET
LIMIT TWO TONS

On a chemist's shop

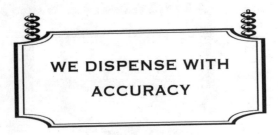

WE DISPENSE WITH
ACCURACY

On a traffic sign

FINE FOR
PARKING
HERE

On a Dublin Bus Nite Link

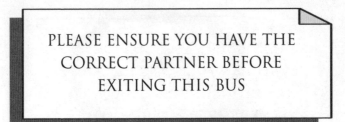

PLEASE ENSURE YOU HAVE THE
CORRECT PARTNER BEFORE
EXITING THIS BUS

At a hospital

MATERNITY
WARD
(NON-ACCIDENT)

In a cemetery

YOU CAN PICK
FLOWERS
ONLY FROM YOUR
OWN GRAVE

At a golf clubhouse

TROUSERS MAY BE WORN BY
LADIES WHILE ON THE COURSE
BUT MUST BE REMOVED
BEFORE ENTERING THE
CLUBHOUSE

In a post office

TO PREVENT PENS BEING STOLEN
NO PENS WILL BE PROVIDED

In a chemist's shop

TRY OUR HEADACHE PILLS
YOU'LL NEVER GET BETTER

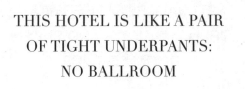

THIS HOTEL IS LIKE A PAIR
OF TIGHT UNDERPANTS:
NO BALLROOM

PLEASE DO NOT USE
THIS LIFT WHEN IT IS
OUT OF ORDER

DRIVE-IN SWIMMING POOL

TO CALL ROOM SERVICE
OPEN THE DOOR AND SHOUT
'ROOM SERVICE'

PLEASE DO NOT LOCK
THIS DOOR AS WE
HAVE LOST THE KEY

THE TV SHOULD BE SWITCHED
ON ONLY WHEN IN USE

PLEASE PRESS THIS
BUTTON FOR MAID
SERVICE
IF NO ANSWER
DO IT YOURSELF

THIS DOOR IS NOT TO BE
USED AS AN ENTRANCE
OR EXIT

ALL FIRE EXTINGUISHERS SHOULD
BE CHECKED AT LEAST A WEEK
BEFORE THE FIRE

IF YOU SMOKE IN BED PLEASE LEAVE
US A FORWARDING ADDRESS TO WHICH
WE CAN SEND THE ASHES

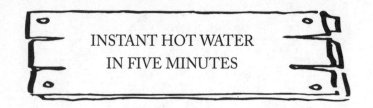

INSTANT HOT WATER
IN FIVE MINUTES

TOILETS:
← SETTERS
POINTERS →

PEOPLE REQUIRING AN EARLY
MORNING ALARM CALL SHOULD
WAKE THE PORTER FIRST

BRIDAL SUITE:
PARTIES CATERED FOR

GUESTS ARE ADVISED
TO TAKE ADVANTAGE OF
THE SERVICES OF THE
CHAMBERMAIDS AFTER
LUNCH

HOTEL SHOP OPEN 24 HOURS
(BUT NOT CONSECUTIVELY)

On a Moore Street stall in Dublin

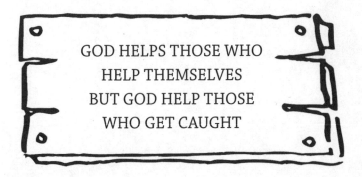

GOD HELPS THOSE WHO
HELP THEMSELVES
BUT GOD HELP THOSE
WHO GET CAUGHT

On the roadside

WELCOME TO
CASTLEBAR
EARLY-CLOSING DAY
ALL DAY THURSDAY

On a card shop

VALENTINE CARDS NOW IN STOCK
IN PACKETS OF TWELVE ONLY

Outside a club

MEMBERS AND
NON-MEMBERS ONLY

On a factory gate

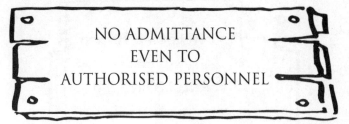

NO ADMITTANCE
EVEN TO
AUTHORISED PERSONNEL

Seen in Cork city

THIS STREET IS A
ONE-WAY CUL-DE-SAC AT
BOTH ENDS

In a holiday village

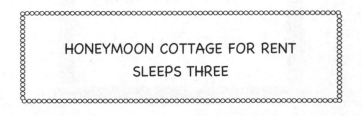

HONEYMOON COTTAGE FOR RENT
SLEEPS THREE

On an antique shop

GENUINE ANTIQUES

– AS NEW

On a road near Killarney

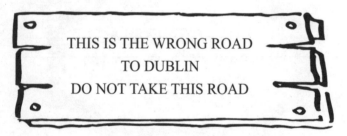

THIS IS THE WRONG ROAD
TO DUBLIN
DO NOT TAKE THIS ROAD

In a home laundry

WHY KILL YOURSELF
WITH WASHING?
LET US DO IT BY HAND

On a dance hall

ENTRANCE IN
ENTRANCE OUT

On a Sligo jail in the nineteenth century

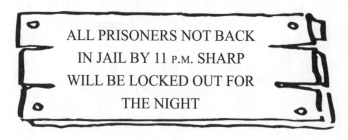

ALL PRISONERS NOT BACK
IN JAIL BY 11 P.M. SHARP
WILL BE LOCKED OUT FOR
THE NIGHT

On the banks of the River Shannon

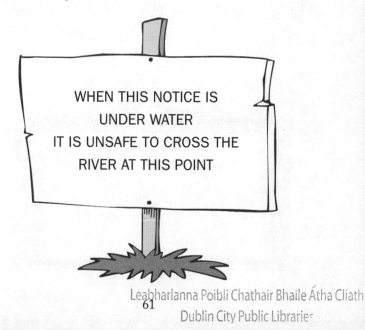

WHEN THIS NOTICE IS
UNDER WATER
IT IS UNSAFE TO CROSS THE
RIVER AT THIS POINT

At a country race meeting

DONKEY RACES
OPEN TO
RESIDENTS
OF THE PARISH
ONLY

On a suburban gate

SALESMEN WELCOME
- DOG FOOD IS EXPENSIVE

On an optician's window

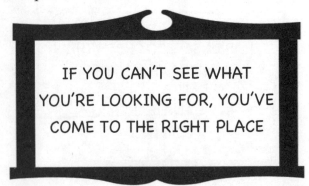

IF YOU CAN'T SEE WHAT
YOU'RE LOOKING FOR, YOU'VE
COME TO THE RIGHT PLACE

THE MAN WHO LENDS
TOOLS IS OUT

THIS IS THE
BEST PLACE
IN TOWN TO
TAKE A LEAK

GET YOUR PETROL
HERE: THE NEXT
THREE GARAGES
ARE MIRAGES

NO APPOINTMENT
NECESSARY TO HAVE A
NEW EXHAUST FITTED.
WE CAN HEAR YOU
COMING

OUR ATTENDANTS
ARE FILLING FINE
TANK YOU

CUSTOMER TOILETS
WIND AND WATER

CAR DAMAGED?
FREE REPAIR ESTIMATES
AT ALMOST NO COST

TRY OUR REPAIR SERVICE AND YOU
WILL NEVER GO ANYWHERE ELSE
AGAIN

LAST PETROL STATION
UNTIL THE NEXT ONE

In a post office

FOR LETTERS TOO LATE
FOR THE NEXT
DELIVERY

On a septic tank truck

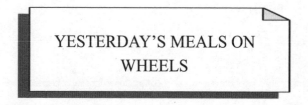

YESTERDAY'S MEALS ON
WHEELS

On another septic tank

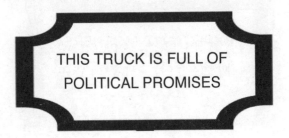

THIS TRUCK IS FULL OF
POLITICAL PROMISES

On yet another septic tank truck

DELIVERIES MONDAY TO FRIDAY ONLY
AT WEEKENDS WE DO THE MILK RUN

*Road sign
near Kildare*

WATER ON ROAD
DURING RAIN

In a Galway bar

EXPECTANT MOTHERS
AND OVER SEVENTIES
LOUNGE

On a Killarney shoe shop

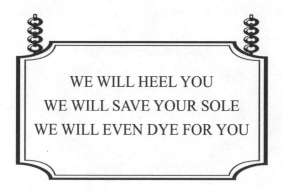

WE WILL HEEL YOU
WE WILL SAVE YOUR SOLE
WE WILL EVEN DYE FOR YOU

Notice carried by a hitchhiker near Athlone

CASH NEEDED FOR
ALCOHOL RESEARCH

In a supermarket

CHOCOLATE BARS
FIVE FOR A EURO,
LIMIT FOUR PER
CUSTOMER

On a Clare cave

WARNING:
CAVES MAY BE
DARK

Road sign in Galway

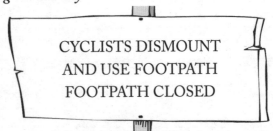

CYCLISTS DISMOUNT
AND USE FOOTPATH
FOOTPATH CLOSED

Notice in a Westport bar

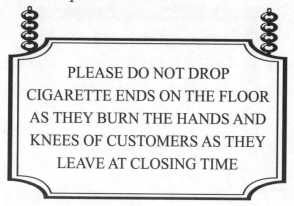

PLEASE DO NOT DROP
CIGARETTE ENDS ON THE FLOOR
AS THEY BURN THE HANDS AND
KNEES OF CUSTOMERS AS THEY
LEAVE AT CLOSING TIME

In a Dublin restaurant

WE WISH TO INFORM CUSTOMERS THAT
THERE IS A 5% EXTRA SERVICE CHARGE TO
COVER THE COST OF COLLECTING THE 10%
SERVICE CHARGE

*A sign seen
in Donegal*

CAUTION
THIS SIGN HAS SHARP EDGES
DO NOT TOUCH THE EDGES OF
THIS SIGN

Seen painted on the back of a car

DON'T LIKE MY DRIVING?
E-MAIL ME @go****yourself.com

On a bakery

WE KNEAD
YOUR
DOUGH

In Cork city

FORMERLY
QUALITY
HOTEL

On a roadside

NO WARNING SIGNALS
ON THIS ROAD

In a shop

ONLY TWO TDS
ALLOWED IN THIS SHOP
AT ANY ONE TIME

On an undertakers

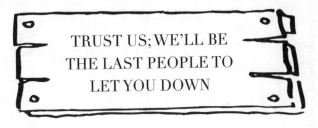

TRUST US; WE'LL BE
THE LAST PEOPLE TO
LET YOU DOWN

On a pet shop

DAY OLD CHICKS
GOING CHEEP

On a well-endowed woman's T-shirt

I WISH THESE WERE BRAINS

In a bar

BEER IS NOW CHEAPER THAN PETROL
DRINK DON'T DRIVE

In a golf clubhouse

ATTENTION GOLFERS
1. Keep your back straight, knees bent and feet shoulder-width apart.
2. Keep your grip loose.
3. Keep your head down.
4. Avoid a quick backswing.
5. Stay out of the water.
6. Try not to hit anyone.
7. If you are delayed, let others go ahead of you.
8. Don't stand directly in front of others.
9. Quiet please while others are in action.

WELL DONE! NOW FLUSH THE
TOILET AND GO PLAY GOLF

In a mental hospital

WE ARE ALL HERE
BECAUSE WE ARE NOT
ALL THERE

On a clinic

THE SLIMMING GROUP MEETS
HERE AT 8 P.M. ON THURSDAYS
PLEASE USE THE LARGE
DOUBLE DOOR AT THE REAR

On an outdoor shop

NOW IS THE
DISCOUNT OF
OUR WINTER
TENT

I WOULD STEP OVER THE BODIES OF TEN NAKED WOMEN TO REACH A PINT OF PORTER

HONEST – I'M DRIVING THIS CAR JUST FOR A BET

IF YOU CAN READ THIS I'VE LOST MY CARAVAN

I'M A BAD DRIVER BUT YOU SHOULD SEE ME PUTT

FORGET THE JONESES I KEEP UP WITH THE SIMPSONS

LOVE THY NEIGHBOUR
BUT DON'T GET CAUGHT

I'M FILTHY STINKING RICH
WELL, TWO OUT OF THREE
ISN'T BAD

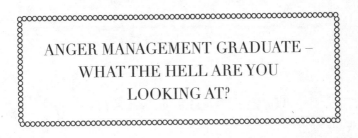

ANGER MANAGEMENT GRADUATE –
WHAT THE HELL ARE YOU
LOOKING AT?

NINE OUT OF TEN OF THE
VOICES IN MY HEAD ARE
SAYING DON'T SHOOT

MY WIFE GIVES SOUND ADVICE
99% SOUND 1% ADVICE

I'VE GOT THE BODY OF AN
EIGHTEEN-YEAR-OLD
IT'S IN THE BOOT

ALASKANS FOR GLOBAL WARMING

ABOLISH HIRE EDUCATION

ALCOHOL IS A SLOW POISON
BUT I'M NOT IN A HURRY

I'M GREAT IN BED –
I CAN SLEEP ALL NIGHT

KEEP HONKING,
I'M RELOADING

I MISSED THE LOTTERY
BY ONLY SIX NUMBERS

IF IT'S THE TOURIST SEASON
WHY CAN'T WE SHOOT THEM?

THANK YOU FOR NOT
LAUGHING AT THIS CAR

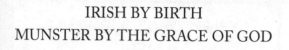

IRISH BY BIRTH
MUNSTER BY THE GRACE OF GOD

BEN THERE
DUNNE THAT
BOUGHT THE TAOISEACH

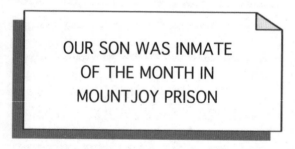

OUR SON WAS INMATE
OF THE MONTH IN
MOUNTJOY PRISON

GIVE ME CHOCOLATE
AND NOBODY GETS HURT

DYSLEXICS OF THE WORLD
UNTIE

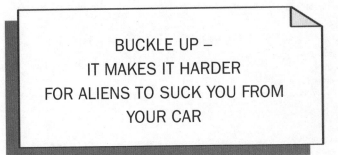

BUCKLE UP –
IT MAKES IT HARDER
FOR ALIENS TO SUCK YOU FROM
YOUR CAR

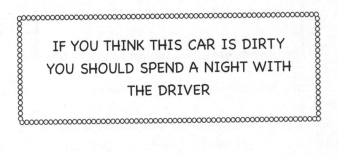

IF YOU THINK THIS CAR IS DIRTY
YOU SHOULD SPEND A NIGHT WITH
THE DRIVER

IT'S NO USE TELLING ME TO
STUFF IT
I'M A TAXIDERMIST

STUPIDITY IS NOT A HANDICAP
PARK SOMEWHERE ELSE

THEY COULDN'T REPAIR MY BRAKES
BUT THEY MADE MY HORN LOUDER

DON'T LAUGH AT THIS CAR
YOUR DAUGHTER MAY BE INSIDE

KERRY FOR YOUR HOLIDAYS
DUBLIN FOR THE ALL-IRELAND

IF YOU CAN READ THIS STICKER
YOU'RE TOO DAMN CLOSE

WHY RISK A HANGOVER?
STAY DRUNK

IF I ACTUALLY GAVE A SHIT
YOU WOULD BE THE FIRST
PERSON I WOULD GIVE IT TO

KEEP DUBLIN CLEAN
DUMP YOUR LITTER IN
THE WICKLOW MOUNTAINS

EVERY THIRTY SECONDS A WOMAN
GIVES BIRTH
WE MUST FIND THIS
WOMAN AND STOP HER

I BELIEVE IN GUN CONTROL
I USE BOTH HANDS

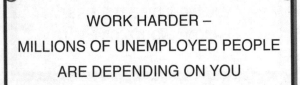

WORK HARDER –
MILLIONS OF UNEMPLOYED PEOPLE
ARE DEPENDING ON YOU

DRIVER HAS NO CASH –
I'M MARRIED

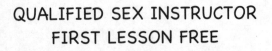

QUALIFIED SEX INSTRUCTOR
FIRST LESSON FREE

NO! NO!! NO!!!
WELL, ALL RIGHT THEN

STOP HONKING OR YOU'LL
WAKE THE GUY IN MY BOOT

THEY USE THE MUSHROOM METHOD
IN OUR COLLEGE –
FEED THE STUDENTS WITH BULLSHIT
AND KEEP THEM IN THE DARK

MARRIAGE HAS CURED MY FEAR
OF BEING ALONE

I'M A VIRGIN
(THIS IS A VERY OLD CAR STICKER)

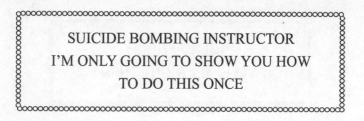

SUICIDE BOMBING INSTRUCTOR
I'M ONLY GOING TO SHOW YOU HOW
TO DO THIS ONCE

I'M NOT A DIRTY OLD MAN
I'M A SEXUALLY ACTIVE
SENIOR CITIZEN

YESTERDAY I GAVE UP DRINKING
TODAY I'M MAKING A COMEBACK

Outside a Cork theatre

SORRY, ALL EMPTY
SEATS ARE FULL

On a building site

SAFETY LADDER
CLIMB AT OWN RISK

In a health food store

SHOPLIFTERS WILL BE BEATEN
OVER THE HEAD WITH AN
ORGANIC CARROT

In Dublin Zoo

PLEASE DO NOT FEED THE ANIMALS
IF YOU HAVE ANY FOOD GIVE IT TO
THE KEEPERS

On an undertakers

PAY NOW – GO LATER

On another undertakers

WE GUARANTEE TO LET
YOU DOWN

On yet another undertakers

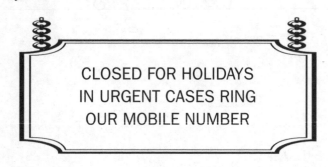

CLOSED FOR HOLIDAYS
IN URGENT CASES RING
OUR MOBILE NUMBER

On a dilapidated shop

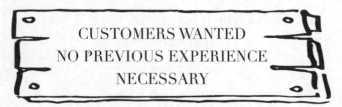

CUSTOMERS WANTED
NO PREVIOUS EXPERIENCE
NECESSARY

On a barber's shop

DURING RENOVATIONS
CUSTOMERS WILL BE
SHAVED IN THE REAR

On a city street corner

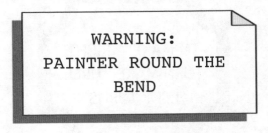

WARNING:
PAINTER ROUND THE
BEND

On a farm

MANURE FOR
SALE

FILL IT YOURSELF
€5 A BAG

On a roadside

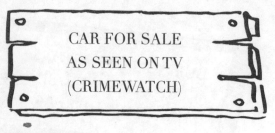

CAR FOR SALE
AS SEEN ON TV
(CRIMEWATCH)

On a road near Cork

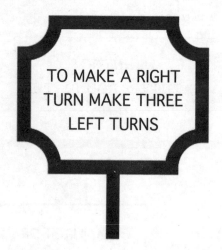

TO MAKE A RIGHT
TURN MAKE THREE
LEFT TURNS

On a public toilet

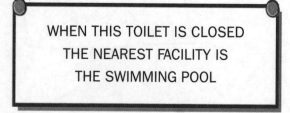

WHEN THIS TOILET IS CLOSED
THE NEAREST FACILITY IS
THE SWIMMING POOL

Road sign in Limerick

EFFIN VILLAGE

On a music shop window

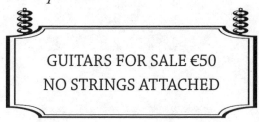

GUITARS FOR SALE €50
NO STRINGS ATTACHED

On a village hall

THE EVENING OF
CLAIRVOYANCE ON
MONDAY NEXT HAS BEEN
CANCELLED
DUE TO UNFORESEEN
CIRCUMSTANCES

On a pylon

WARNING!
TO TOUCH THESE WIRES MEANS
INSTANT DEATH, ANYONE DOING
SO WILL BE PROSECUTED

On a sheep farm

DOGS FOUND WORRYING
WILL BE SHOT

Near a lake

ANY PERSON PASSING
BEYOND THIS POINT
WILL BE DROWNED
BY ORDER OF THE
URBAN COUNCIL

On a town hall

THOUSANDS EXPECTED
AT OUR NEXT DANCE
(HALL CAPACITY 500)

On a school gate

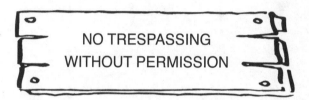

NO TRESPASSING
WITHOUT PERMISSION

In an office

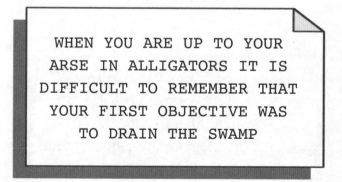

WHEN YOU ARE UP TO YOUR
ARSE IN ALLIGATORS IT IS
DIFFICULT TO REMEMBER THAT
YOUR FIRST OBJECTIVE WAS
TO DRAIN THE SWAMP

On a suburban house

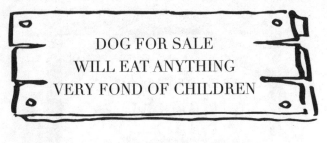

DOG FOR SALE
WILL EAT ANYTHING
VERY FOND OF CHILDREN

In Belfast city

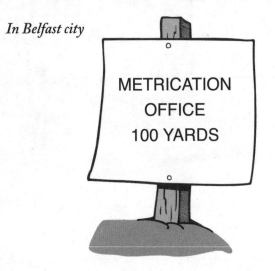

METRICATION
OFFICE
100 YARDS

In a barber's shop

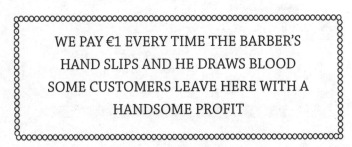

WE PAY €1 EVERY TIME THE BARBER'S
HAND SLIPS AND HE DRAWS BLOOD
SOME CUSTOMERS LEAVE HERE WITH A
HANDSOME PROFIT

In a cemetery

THIS STONE WAS
ERECTED TO THE
MEMORY OF
MIKE McCARTHY
WHO WAS DROWNED
IN THE LAKES OF
KILLARNEY BY A FEW OF
HIS DEAREST FRIENDS

On the old Capitol Cinema in Grand Parade

CLOSING DOWN
THANKS TO THE
PEOPLE OF CORK

On a country estate

PLEASE DO
NOT DEFACE
THIS NOTICE

In a newspaper

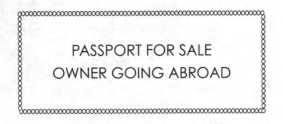

PASSPORT FOR SALE
OWNER GOING ABROAD

Near Sligo

**PLEASE DO NOT STEAL
THIS NOTICE**

(Within a couple of days it was gone!)

In Dublin Zoo

LOST CHILDREN WILL BE
TAKEN TO THE LION HOUSE

On a truck

RUBBISH REMOVED
SATISFACTION GUARANTEED
OR TWICE YOUR
GARBAGE BACK

On an antique shop

*ENGLISH SPOKEN
AMERICAN
UNDERSTOOD*

On a travel agents

PLEASE GO AWAY

On a farm

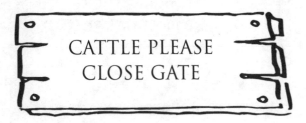

CATTLE PLEASE
CLOSE GATE

Seen in Galway

FOOTPATH
UNSUITABLE FOR
PEDESTRIANS

In Cork railway station

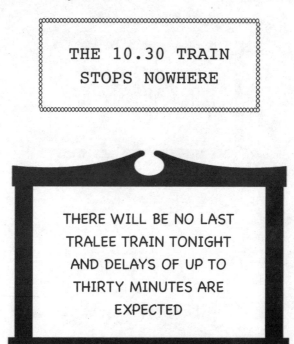

THE 10.30 TRAIN
STOPS NOWHERE

THERE WILL BE NO LAST
TRALEE TRAIN TONIGHT
AND DELAYS OF UP TO
THIRTY MINUTES ARE
EXPECTED

In Kinsale

CORK 19
HALF-WAY 9½

In a doctor's waiting-room

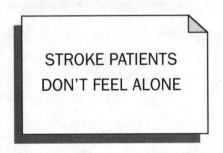

STROKE PATIENTS
DON'T FEEL ALONE

In a garden centre

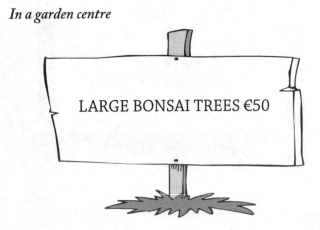

LARGE BONSAI TREES €50

Seen on a ladder at a building site

LAST RUNG
PLEASE STOP

In a public park

NO PERSON SHALL RUN,
PLAY GAMES, CYCLE OR
LIE ON THE GRASS IN
THIS PLEASURE GROUND

THE MINISTER FOR FINANCE
WILL ADDRESS A PUBLIC
MEETING AT THIS VENUE ON
SATURDAY NEXT
BEWARE OF PICKPOCKETS

In a maternity hospital

VISITING HOURS 8 P.M. TO 9 P.M.
HUSBANDS ONLY
ONE PER PATIENT

At a summer fête

ENTRIES FOR
THE BABY SHOW
MUST BE
HANDED IN AT
THE GATE

On a newly painted park bench

WET PAINT
WATCH IT OR WEAR IT

At a pedestrian crossing

WAIT FOR THE GREEN
MAN TO CROSS

In a chemist's shop

INSECTS COMING
INTO CONTACT WITH
THIS SPRAY DIE
WITHOUT HOPE OF
RECOVERY

On a laser machine

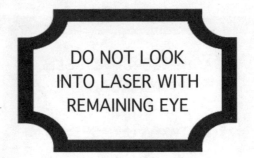

DO NOT LOOK
INTO LASER WITH
REMAINING EYE

In a factory

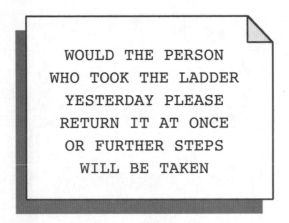

WOULD THE PERSON
WHO TOOK THE LADDER
YESTERDAY PLEASE
RETURN IT AT ONCE
OR FURTHER STEPS
WILL BE TAKEN

On a bottle of hair restorer

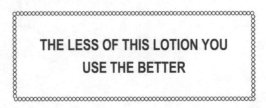

THE LESS OF THIS LOTION YOU
USE THE BETTER

In a railway station

PASSENGERS ARE ASKED
NOT TO CROSS THE
LINES
IT TAKES US AGES TO
UNCROSS THEM AGAIN

On a circus

MAN WANTED AS HUMAN
CANNONBALL
MUST BE WILLING TO
TRAVEL

On a school gate

FUND-RAISING JUMBLE SALE
BRING SOMETHING YOU
DON'T NEED
WIVES BRING YOUR
HUSBANDS

In a Dublin university

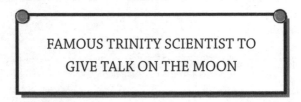

FAMOUS TRINITY SCIENTIST TO
GIVE TALK ON THE MOON

In a school cloakroom

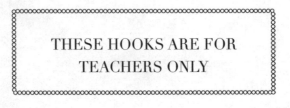

THESE HOOKS ARE FOR
TEACHERS ONLY

On an undertakers

NOBODY HAVING ONCE
TRIED ONE OF OUR
COFFINS WILL EVER USE
ANY OTHER

In a police station

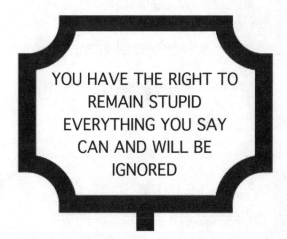

YOU HAVE THE RIGHT TO
REMAIN STUPID
EVERYTHING YOU SAY
CAN AND WILL BE
IGNORED

At a railway station

THE REAR
PORTION OF
THE TRAIN
WILL NOT RUN
TONIGHT

In a dentist's surgery

PAIN FREE
WE CHARGE FOR
EVERYTHING ELSE

In a supermarket

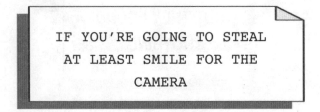

IF YOU'RE GOING TO STEAL
AT LEAST SMILE FOR THE
CAMERA

On a packet of sleeping tablets

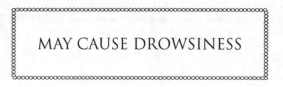

MAY CAUSE DROWSINESS

On a butcher's shop

PLEASED TO MEET YOU
MEAT TO PLEASE YOU

On a truck

I HAD A BRAIN SCAN
BUT THEY FOUND
NOTHING

On a minibus

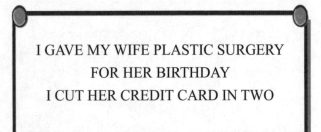

I GAVE MY WIFE PLASTIC SURGERY
FOR HER BIRTHDAY
I CUT HER CREDIT CARD IN TWO

On a family planning clinic

DURING REPAIRS
WILL CUSTOMERS
PLEASE USE THE
REAR ENTRANCE

On a plumber's van

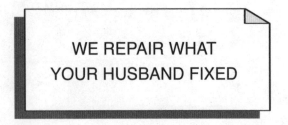

WE REPAIR WHAT
YOUR HUSBAND FIXED

On a shop

FAMILY BUTCHER

On a box of Christmas lights

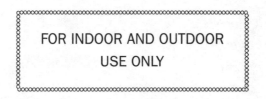

FOR INDOOR AND OUTDOOR
USE ONLY

In a housing estate

HOUSE TO LET
FOUR BEDROOMS
LARGE BATHROOM (AT
PRESENT OCCUPIED BY
OWNER)

In a boarding house

NO SOLIDS IN
DOWNSTAIRS
TOILET PLEASE

Outside a butcher's shop

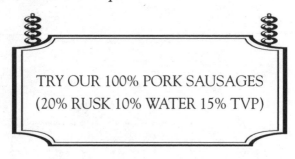

TRY OUR 100% PORK SAUSAGES
(20% RUSK 10% WATER 15% TVP)

Advertisement in a newspaper

HEARSE FOR SALE
NEW ENGINE
ORIGINAL BODY

Sign on a psychologist's door

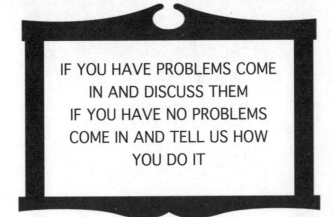

IF YOU HAVE PROBLEMS COME
IN AND DISCUSS THEM
IF YOU HAVE NO PROBLEMS
COME IN AND TELL US HOW
YOU DO IT

Sign in a restaurant

SHOES ARE REQUIRED
TO EAT IN THIS
RESTAURANT

Underneath someone had scribbled:
SOCKS CAN EAT WHEREVER THEY WANT!

In a hotel

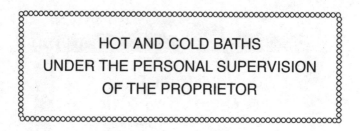

HOT AND COLD BATHS
UNDER THE PERSONAL SUPERVISION
OF THE PROPRIETOR

In a bank

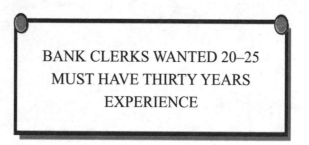

BANK CLERKS WANTED 20–25
MUST HAVE THIRTY YEARS
EXPERIENCE

On a maternity hospital

DELIVERIES
AT REAR

On a dance hall

UNACCOMPANIED LADIES NOT ADMITTED WITHOUT MALE COMPANION

Near a school

SLOW CHILDREN

On a garage

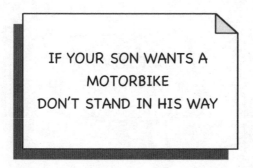

IF YOUR SON WANTS A MOTORBIKE DON'T STAND IN HIS WAY

On a farm

FOR SALE
INDIVIDUALLY LAID
EGGS

In a department store

*KID GLOVES FOR SALE
TO FIT ANY SIZE KID*

In a jeweller's shop

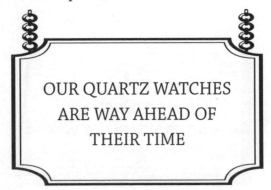

OUR QUARTZ WATCHES
ARE WAY AHEAD OF
THEIR TIME

In a church

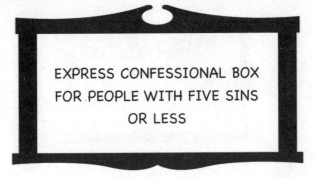

EXPRESS CONFESSIONAL BOX
FOR PEOPLE WITH FIVE SINS
OR LESS

In a restaurant

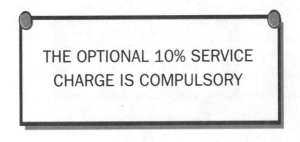

THE OPTIONAL 10% SERVICE
CHARGE IS COMPULSORY

On a factory

MULLIGAN'S TOOL
WORKS

Newspaper advertisement

FOR SALE
LEOPARDSKIN COAT
SPOTLESS

Road sign near Belfast

YOU ARE NOW
APPROACHING
THE END OF THIS
ROUNDABOUT

In a pub toilet

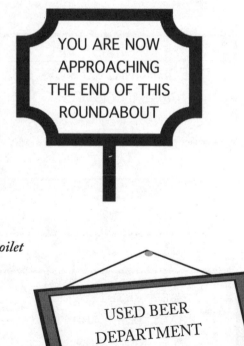

USED BEER
DEPARTMENT

In a church hall

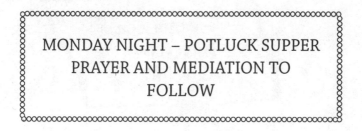

MONDAY NIGHT – POTLUCK SUPPER
PRAYER AND MEDIATION TO
FOLLOW

In a church

WE NOW HAVE FONTS AT
THE TOP AND BOTTOM OF
THE CHURCH
BABIES WILL BE
BAPTISED AT BOTH ENDS

In a shop

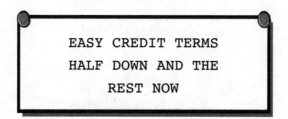

EASY CREDIT TERMS
HALF DOWN AND THE
REST NOW

In a pub

HAVE ANOTHER DRINK
YOUR WIFE CAN ONLY GET
SO MAD

On a dress shop

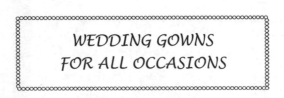

*WEDDING GOWNS
FOR ALL OCCASIONS*

Near an undertakers

PARKING FOR
CLIENTS ONLY

On a church notice board

THIS WEEK'S SERMON WILL
BE 'WHAT IS HELL?'
COME EARLY AND LISTEN TO
THE CHOIR PRACTICE

In a parish bulletin

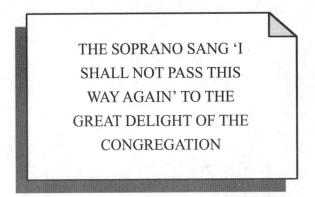

THE SOPRANO SANG 'I
SHALL NOT PASS THIS
WAY AGAIN' TO THE
GREAT DELIGHT OF THE
CONGREGATION

Sign on a government building

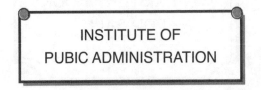

INSTITUTE OF
PUBIC ADMINISTRATION

Notice painted on the road

**WARNING
SHCOOL AHEAD**

In a railway station

BEWARE OF TRAINS
GOING BOTH WAYS

On a bookshop

SECOND HAND, RARE,
OUT-OF-PRINT AND
NON-EXISTENT BOOKS
FOR SALE

Near a McDonalds in Dublin

PARKING FOR
DRIVE-THROUGH
CUSTOMERS ONLY

On a dry-cleaners

WE HAVE BEEN TWENTY
YEARS ON THE SAME
SPOT

On a garage

WE SUPPLY PETROL TO
ANY MOTORIST IN A
PLASTIC CAN

On a building society

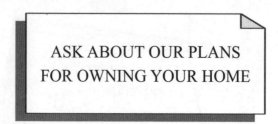

ASK ABOUT OUR PLANS
FOR OWNING YOUR HOME

On a school wastepaper basket

EMPTY
WHEN
FULL

On a junk shop

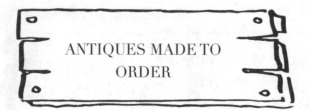

ANTIQUES MADE TO
ORDER

On a restaurant

THE EARLY BIRD GETS
THE WORM
BREAKFAST SERVED
UNTIL 10 A.M.

On a Cork street

THE CORK DOGS HOME

Underneath was written:

I DIDN'T EVEN KNOW HE'D BEEN AWAY

In a beauty shop

BUY OUR PERFUME –
YOU KNOW IT MAKES
SCENTS

On a shop

GUNS AND WEDDING RINGS

On an antique shop

GENUINE FAKE
ANTIQUES

*On a banana stand
in Dublin's Moore Street*

EXOTIC
CURVED
YELLOW FRUIT
50 CENT EACH

Over a pub toilet

INTERNATIONAL TOILETS

GOING IN – RUSSIAN
INSIDE – EUROPEAN
GOING OUT – FINNISH

On a country pub

BIG DICK'S
HALFWAY INN

Sign seen near Killarney

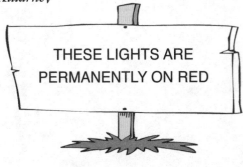

THESE LIGHTS ARE
PERMANENTLY ON RED

Road sign in County Clare

SIXMILEBRIDGE
THREE MILES

On a Galway jeweller's shop

CUSTOMERS – COME IN
AND HAVE YOUR THINGS
ENGRAVED

Also available from Mercier Press by the same author

From some of the most celebrated figures of the Emerald Isle, such as Samuel Beckett, Dave Allen and Ardal O'Hanlon, this book brings together a collection of wit, humour and Irish wisdom that may at times seem confusing, but is always profound.

978 1 85635 461 5
RRP €9.99

Cork has its own inimitable brand of humour – as distinctive as the River Lee or the Bells of Shandon. This collection, assembled over many years of listening and learning to appreciate the subtlety and genius of Cork humour, illustrates that humour at its best. Those new to Cork are in for a treat, and those not new to Cork don't know the half of it!

978 1 85635 565 0
RRP €9.99

The Bumper Book of Kerryman Jokes contains hundreds of jokes, riddles, one-liners, stories and inventions to thrill even the most politically correct among us.

978 1 85635 470 7
RRP €9.99